CALIFORNIA BETWEEN THE FIRES

Poems 2020-2021

CALIFORNIA BETWEEN THE FIRES

Poems 2020-2021

RYAN KENNETH ALLEN

Cover design and photo by Ryan Kenneth Allen.

ryankallen.com

ISBN 978-1-7356364-3-6

CALIFORNIA BETWEEN THE FIRES

Poems 2020-2021

RYAN KENNETH ALLEN

Cover design and photo by Ryan Kenneth Allen.

ryankallen.com

ISBN 978-1-7356364-3-6

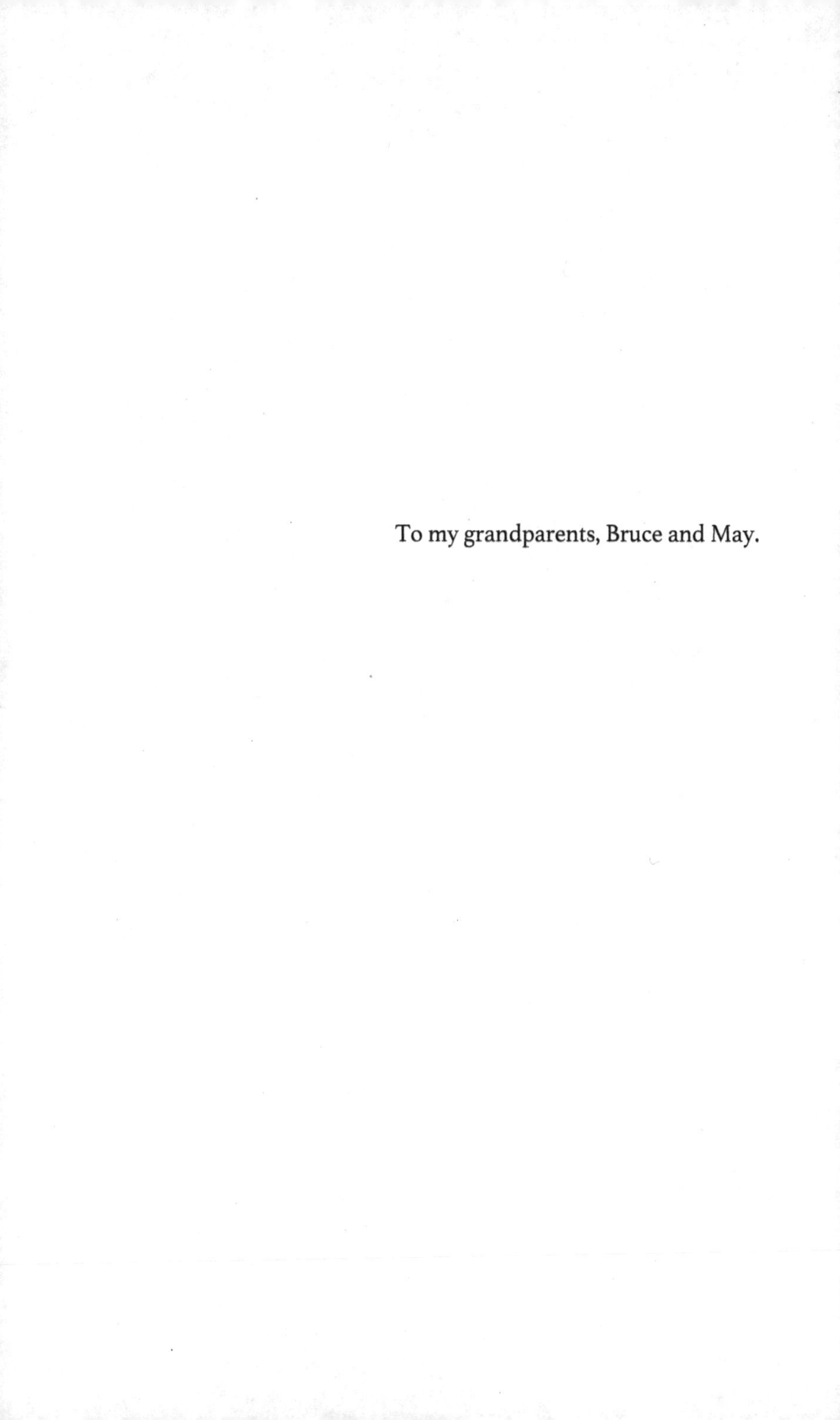

To my grandparents, Bruce and May.

CONTENTS

A MOURNING

A HISTORY

AGAINST THE EVENING

The ceiling beams rising from the southeastern wall
always reach the apex. My heart beats out of my chest.
The keys rest willingly beneath my fingertips, but tonight
moving them is like threading a nut onto a rusted bolt.
My heart beats out of my chest and mostly my fingers
lie still. I struggle to impart a rhythm through the hammering
and through the steady brightening of the kitchen light
against the evening. Each beam strikes the peak
one by one. I hear each impact—ping! ping! ping!—
like iron on iron, and my heart beats out of my chest.

When we found the wagon wheel half-buried in the muck
of the exposed lakebed, the wood seemed the color of nightfall.
The wagon wheel at first, then slowly there were
other small pieces, splintered and waterlogged,
softened with rot and a hundred odd years of settling
into mud that once held other boots than ours and spoke of
losses cut, belongings left, the ageless pull to turn and ride
against the evening. Mud under hoofbeats, bootfalls,
summer-dry or winter-wet or sometimes seemingly both
and unending, unending under foot and iron-wrapped oak
or ash.

My brother's camcorder caught the years sunk into that wood
and the seconds as they ticked past around us but without
our knowing, and one day I might ask him if the footage has

survived, over several moves and amid a new, electronic decay,
on some years-motionless drive, waiting to replace
our blurred and sepia-toned memories of childhood with its
single, digital perspective. I remember we left the wagon wheel,
and when we left it, it was gone with all the lack of dwelling
and forward-and-onward with which children advance
against the evening, even if by then we were years beyond
childhood in self-consideration and well on our way to
rippling, societal adulthood. We advanced to a narrow channel
snaking between the lakeshore and a small island revealed
by the drought's insatiable draw on the waterline. We thought
we could jump it, the gap narrow and we beyond childhood,
but none among us could, so we resumed the given path
behind our father, our shoes now soaked and steps now
plodding, toward some other evening's camp.

I close my laptop and scratch a few unsteady words
on the back of a page as the evening reaches nightfall,
the pen and the paper hammering no rhythm in their
concert, though their impact rings like iron on iron
against the evening and against my heart beating out of my
chest and the wagon wheel lying under snowmelt and muck
between the droughts, and one of these beams will be
the first to rot or splinter, paint-peeling in burning April,
struck by the insatiable draw of the waterline or
as I am struck, like waterlogged sneakers crunching
on uneven rocks which break apart the dirt.

DAVIS

I

The warming spring air and the deep-green grass of the quad
shone like childhood summer through the library windows,
but I couldn't stand it.

As Netflix rolled the next episode of *Lost*, I glanced at the clock
to figure out how many more episodes I could squeeze in
before the last bus left.

Probably three,
there was a bus stop just around
the corner.

Someone tossed a frisbee on the quad
and I angled my laptop away from the window.
I drank until I collapsed.

A year earlier, during the height of the Occupy movement—
when the tents didn't just dapple the campus quad and Central Park,
they dominated them—
the university police pepper sprayed some students
on the walkway between the library and the Memorial Union.

For a while afterward you could still see the stains on the pavement,
but eventually those faded too.
Now it was only lovely.

Five o'clock came and I pushed the door open
into the cooling evening.

It was Saturday and I could live forever.

II

I found myself at an outdoor table
near one of the buildings—science or math—
in which I'd never had a class as a student.

The heat was becoming bearable
as the day slid toward an early-summer sunset,
and the light sweat I'd worked up
during a sweetly nostalgic tour of campus
began its slow abatement.

It had been long enough that the anxious dreams
of missed exams and classrooms I couldn't find
had finally reached a halt.

I knew they weren't good times,
but many a past finds an alluring glow
when the seas ahead look bleak.

It was eight P.M. before she was out of surgery,
and it turned out this was it.

The sidewalk slowly darkened as I walked
a familiar path back to my car.

The speed bumps in the parking garage
rocked the cab over blackwater pavement.

My headlights shone the way the bikes surged
when spring finally mounted, but I turned right
and drove away in darkness.

TRAVELING ALONE

She asked me if I thought I was a martyr.
Of course I was taken aback, the question not met
with an immediate dismissal only because
the idea was so utterly foreign.

Imagine traveling alone through a vast desert in the night—
everything moon-blue like a dream or like nostalgia, warm sepia,
the color of a place where you can only be alone—
when you hear the rasping inquiry, "¿Se piensa mártir?"

and you, startled by this voice without a face
and, for the sake of argument, knowing nothing
of Spanish but perhaps, "¿Cómo está?" and, "Me llamo Pablo,"
and not even certain that it *was* Spanish

except for your faint recognition of the accent—
you being from California and having lived your life
within the intermingling of cultures—you are expected
to have an answer, but all you want right now

is to make some progress across the ageless sand
while the night is cool and welcoming and before the sun
resumes its brutal lashing at your back, driving you onward
though you need not its savage encouragement.

That your tale might live for others to tell is stripped
like the sweat from your skin by the merciless oven
before you can reap its ounce of relief,
and soon you forget that voice in the sand.

There may be others, there may have been others—
you forget them all in turn.
Imagine traveling alone.

The book we were discussing is nothing but the mess of youth.
I laughed and said,
“No, surely not.”

EIGHTY-SIX AND WINDY

I try to figure which side of the tree I am,
when the wind swirls just one side but not the other,
leaves all in a flurry or untouched, suspended,
and returned to amnion.

As I attempt to saddle myself
to something woody, or something green,
the parking lot is less a contrast than I'd have hoped,
were I, by nature, one to hope.
Less distinct is the line between earth and our anointed artifice,
all concrete and steel and new, always just as new—
this sidewalk that leads not to a nearby cedar,
as it seemed at first, but just past it
and arcs, engineered and perfect, through the grass
with an unexpected grace, like there's a certain value
in the paved and trampled, like these blades,
these bracts, and this bark that know no uncertainty.
And so I think, *maybe I'm not*
the tree at all.

I think, *am I the wind itself,*
lifting dust and carving mountains in my likeness?
Though textbooks would tell me it's not the wind
that carves them, and they were, in fact, not carved at all
but thrust from underneath with a violence
stretched beyond our perception.

So what am I left? Lifting dust? Lifting dust
and leveling houses and shouldering a surge beyond the seawall?
There's much destruction left in the lifting of dust,
in the ushering of flames through the canyon,
and, *it's a shame*, I think, *that this selfsame breeze*
can brush my skin and bring relief and peace so that I forgive it.
But the world is full of shame, and between the gusts
the sweat from my brow is left to build above imperceptible—
uncomfortable, even just sitting. *But at least*, I think,
at least I'm not the wind.

I think that while I am none of these things—
not the wind, the leaves on either side, and not the tree itself—
I am stirring just the same.

Call my biopic *Eighty-Six and Windy*, or
California Between the Fires.

HIGHWAY FLAMES

Black smoke rises in a twist beside
the telephone poles at the horizon.
A minute later we pass the orange
diamond. "Wreck ahead," it warns.

When we reach the truck, the flames
have eaten metal down to black and gray
and not much left of the front
of the trailer. Men stand by and
wet the grass to keep the tongues
of flame confined to Sherwin-Williams
cargo. The scene is calm and we agree,
"They must have gotten out all right."

We pass the held-up traffic in the
northbound lane, regain our speed,
and watch the slender dust devils
dance like ghostly paper lanterns
over miles of scattered sagebrush
to the west.

A SUGGESTION

HOME

Sometimes, in the milky-soft light
of the waning dawn,
those few steps out to the parking lot
are a different place.

They paved the path between
scenes of sleek blacks, off-whites,
and all the different names for brown,
but the pavement isn't where my eyes are drawn.

The sky is hardly different
from the shadows of buildings and trees,
but it's there, no longer blue,
grayed by the drifting smoke
of thunderstorm wildfires,
but the sky isn't where my eyes are drawn.

My eyes are underneath the air,
and when I see, I see it filtered
blue and purple, deep, subtle,
suspended in the warming softness.

It's the only part of the day
that doesn't exist.

It's only moment slipping
into moment.

Nothing stops, nothing pushes
to lean over the rail.

The wind whips the spray of the sea
against my face where it will,
the waves roll back,
and perhaps we'll meet again.

The car door pulls me
back above the air.
I breathe the gray
and try to stop my beating heart.

The sea was never there.

The place I left, the place I'll go—
I struggle to decide which of these is home.
I turn the key to drown
myself in noise.

The sea was never there.

A DEATH

The way a folding chair sits in the middle of an empty room
is rigid, all utility with nothing (read: *no one*)
to benefit. A chair is a chair is a chair is what
I keep telling myself. The angles, the structure, the
plastic and metal—what else? What else if not a chair?
Well, plastic and metal and rivets (see: *metal*)
fashioned to hold their collective shape long enough
to portray a familiar permanence. Really it's
a semi-permanence; every minute piece remains in motion,
reality betraying stillness over and over and over
in an endless chain of *overs*. Even underutilized, a chair
will experience the breaking down of all things—a death,
if you like. But at some point before then, during
or just before or after some undefinable slice of time,
that rigid conglomeration, all utility and nothing else,
sitting in the middle (dramatic: *epicenter*) of an empty room,
will cease to be a chair. Emptiness is the death
of familiarity. A chair is a chair is a chair is what
I keep telling myself.

BETWEEN THE RAINS

A miracle would be the rain's return to California.

Real rain. Rain like early barely-memories
of stacking sandbags in front of the house in Dayton.

Rains that threaten—but *just* threaten—to burst the dam,
exposing one more piece of our hubris.

We've had enough of this one.

TRAMPLED GRASSES

Would that I could put pen to paper
in a manner befitting the morning radiance,
here within this valley of life, here beside
this lake not yet hidden by guardian hills
which but strive for mountainhood.

How many thousands of years
will the summer flies buzz with thawed urgency
around and against the salt of our brow—
left perhaps from midnight roiling,
perhaps from yesterday's sun—
to upset this gentle forum of calling birds
and cicadas ringing into disagreement?

I escape to tented nylon,
envision permanent asylum
in plaster, wood, and glass, a peace in which
to strike the morning dew upon the page
in a manner befitting its ghostly dawn accretion
but to find my brow beset by voices of my own
and no agreeing forum, no mounted mitigation.

Would that I could recall the morning
now escaped. Our afternoon is trampled
grasses overthrown.

REFLECTIONS

I said, "No, I don't think you were the one to mess this all up,"
because you were shining like the sun on down to me, and maybe
someday we could face the same direction like we knew
what we were doing, where we were going, but then you said
something that I missed—because it was too quiet, or because
I couldn't stand to hear it just then—and we left the water's edge,
striding now unevenly back to your truck, and drove back
across the dam that would almost break several years later, and I said,
"I don't think this is any different than it was before,"
but every day was different to you and you just wanted to get back,
not before dark but before the dark finished soaking up
all the muggy summer warmth, and I've always had trouble
reconciling the passage of time.

FREIGHT

You should know what it's like to live beside a highway,
to be drifting off, your heartbeat finally settling
between a day you didn't want and a morning that won't wait,
only to rouse from half a dream to the distant wail of the train.

It's late, and the conductor keeps the horn to a minimum—
no doubt well aware of that fleeting stillness of the heart—
but you live just for that unconsciousness,
a precious state of mind so precarious that the mere anticipation
of the growing rumble as the train draws nearer
is enough to blow it all up.

Fox in the henhouse—
everything is feathers.

You should know that the next few hours are ruined.
Years down the road you will turn to your smartphone
and drown out the dreadful thumping in your chest
with artificial sweetener, but right now it's 2011,
and though smartphones are no longer the exception,
yours still flips open only to reveal how long it's been
since you last had a real conversation.

You should know this broken silence.
You should have to reckon with this priceless vase
tipped accidentally to the hard tile floor.

Whoever tipped it didn't mean it—really they didn't.
But all you care about right now is that you won't get the vase back
and that even though the train is long gone,
the cars on the highway don't stop,
and you can listen to each one whoosh by if you want.

For some reason you seem to want to.
You should have to wonder why that is.

ALT COUNTRY HILLS

You should listen to alt country
as your tires cut microscopic ruts
in the highway rolling through the hills.
Much more rubber is lost than asphalt—

> no longer are the days of arced wood
> carving through the dust; we strive
> to bear a load the earth cannot—

but the tires have the numbers.
Thousands bound for places soon
to be forgotten. You should let the melody
slowly ease your mind from the pounding,
thrumming progress, the anxious murmur
of artificial veins, as the violins
and strummed guitars play magic
with the rippling grass so you'd swear
you could hear each blade brush its twin,
rasping out its love or its lament.
Alt country because you're looking
not for those things which everyone sees,
not the mainstream patterns of the blurring leaves,
but the small patch of orange poppies—

> which the romantic in you wants to call
> a grove, but you think you could count
> the brush strokes it would take to capture the scene,
> and right now you're sure a grove
> is something somehow immeasurable—

and the tiny saplings beneath the burned-out trees,

the trees that everyone knows now
only as a tragedy—but where was their regard
before the ashy ruin?—

saplings that will live decades yet
before paying homage to their towering
ancestral beauty. But riding through these hills
you think you might just have decades
to spare. And as one sweet song
drifts into another, you should wonder
why that is not always the case.

SPRING

You should watch the buds race
to best the blooming of the day.
Sit within the hanging stillness,
the timeless rests amid the notes
of a bird you'll never see.
You should watch the green arise
as if it never was and rush upon
the air as if it never will again.
Sit beneath the sun and lie
with intervals of rain, a rain
which, so softened in its contact
by the gently peace of letting go,
is cool and clean like no hand ever was.
The growing warmth is not about
the thirst you feel. The widening
of life is not about your means.
There is quiet yearning in places
you will never reach. You should smell
the lawlessness of spring.

A LANDSCAPE

THE MOUNTAIN

The mountain cries the cry of a hawk—
a sound that travels so much further
in the coolness of altitude.

It makes land like a sudden winter gust,
buffeting the parts of me left exposed,
causing me first to hunker against
the frigid imposition.

Second I am beckoned.

THUNDERCLAP

I let the world hit me
like a thunderclap.
The collision is a lightning flash,
and the uneven rumble
rolls through my body.

I used to count the seconds.
Now I listen to the very end
and try to trace its shape.
A piece of something far away
has now become a part of me.

What dust has shaken loose?
Which stones are firmly set?
Which hills caught fire?

I listen, and I find
that each thunderclap
is not the death it seemed at first.

I listen to the rumble,
the rolling shape of something new.

And I used to count the seconds.
Now I listen to the very end.

BREAKING

Just outside the door the great ticking stops
and the heat at my brow melts away on the breeze.

The distant sound of thunder becomes the rumble of hunger,
no longer a rattling in my chest.

With each flash and pause, my body cools,
degree by degree—though here beneath the evening rain,

nothing is measured.

Rain in late May is wonder itself.

How many evenings have I missed,
fever-hot and eyes wide in tense stillness,

striving for the relief found tonight so simply
in these broken gray clouds?

Sweet wonder, cool wonder,
I am awash and breaking.

CALIFORNIA MAY

Each flash of lightning wipes me clean. The effect
is not unique; several neighbors have ambled
likewise to their doorsteps—faces raised in exaltation,
tasting petrichor—to witness each brief glimpse of
daylit clouds, a common sight at noon but a rolling
wonder in evening instants. The rain is now a
chorus, as rain can only sing in California May,
a cooling cloth wrapped against the mounting summer
fever. Likewise I am broken, and if reverence could
burst my chest and rise, now I would be done,
for I am calm enough and clean, laid bare before
each flash of evening sun.

BELONGING

Start me over. This time
use the green of the daylily grass
and the pink of the Indian hawthorn.

Use the gray-brown split-bark
of the sugar maple underneath.
Let the stumbling billbug retrace my

silhouette. All these things
know where they should be. I ask humbly
for their hidden lemon-yellow when

this time I begin.

RESPITE

I can't feel my hands as I drift back into consciousness
having joyously lost twenty minutes of late-April early evening—
or has five o'clock already become late afternoon as we slip,
also joyously, toward May?

The breeze testing the bounds of gentle against the leaves outside
masterfully disguises the soft hums and whirs of traffic,
a lovely static played beneath the pins and needles in my arms
as I lower my hands from their brief crooked respite behind my head.

Catching the little triangle of sky through the front window,
the wedge of blue flanked by trees whose leaves are made
somehow golden by the light of almost sunset, I think
this easing gradient of black drifting into blue and washing into yellow
should be plastered across the walls
of all coming to consciousness.

SLIDING

It's warm—hot really, but warm
because the sun is sliding—
everything is sliding lately—
sliding toward, sliding down,
sliding into—and the breeze is
light. It's an hour till sunset
and everything is open. The day
is not specific. Dragonflies
flit by and move on, do not linger.
The leaves sigh as intermittent
waves without a tempo. The sky
is full and silky blue and I
am scattered over time.

LETTER TO THE COMING SEASON

Hark! This blasted bough belongs to us!
This lightning-stricken wound that clubbed our limb
has halted all advance upon the windward front.

Loosed without delay, the precious golden sap
in store for such disasters kept the insect germ
from spreading plague beneath the bark,
but now we hear the winter come to prey upon our losses.

If it be true that we are left insufficient in accounting,
has yet the season slipped too late to seed once more
in double-effort to retain this priceless footing?

Alas! It must be true, for the rains began a fortnight!
How soon until we wake to find what stand we make
against the frosty morn! And yet, I beg,
do not delay advancement on account of fickle chance.

If fall we must, let not it be in vain before the sun.

Sincerely yours.

We hope to meet in health
when spring has come.

OUT OF DARKNESS

This is a spindly pine
that has pushed its veins skyward
over eight years of snow and sun.

These are its young, round cones
in extended constellation,
held in delicate repose before
their destined blackward spiral.

These brown depths propel creation
in strands of unseen silk.

Out of darkness light is thrust.

THAT GENTLE WHITE

I

One wispy cotton puff hung in the sky,
suspended in the distance as if preserved
in a clear resin sphere on a fourth-floor desk,
unmoving at a glance, which is all it's ever given.

All the world in an easy, feathery unraveling,
heaped with inbox novelty and the slow abandonment
of day becoming day becoming day.
Heaped.

II

Yesterday that gentle white
hung but for a moment.

Yet today I close my eyes
and see it hanging as it did.

O what it is that we have
unknowingly in our possession.

NEVADA

I see her eyes in the hills of Nevada,
where the dusty carpet of sage reaches its fingers
up the gentle, tanned slopes
surrounding the high desert.

Without any trees to break the landscape,
every cloud-thrown shadow is visible,
their slow creep across the valleys
lost in the streaking highway miles.

It's land we only ever touch in transit.

The hills open to sparse farmland,
plots of manufactured green cut by
lively yellow grass.

It's this grass I'll dream of later,

between days of halting travel.
Dreams the color of life
to fill the cracks.

GOLD BEACH

The Oregon coast in April, and the sky
is amazingly sunny. Windy, of course, so
you're still sent reaching for a sweater
to sit for any length in the shade. It's
weather you can't ask for, and the last
two days the clouds returned and we drove
by the bar and grill in Gold Beach with
"Congratulations Class of 2018" painted
black and silent on the wall.
Next time this and next time that,
we say.

A MOURNING

IDAHO

I give my love the sugar beet fields of Idaho,
squat green rows with hardly space
for feet to dance or trudge between them. Flat,
these fields for miles are given up to God,
who, gazing down in blue expanse,
provides to those who toil.

I give my love the flight of the swallowtail.
So still am I to not disturb,
as insects drink the sweat from my skin.
Is it not God who hands it all to us? The
pure white billows atop the sunlit clouds
can be but heaven boiling over the mountains to the west.

I give of children running, the innocence in roses,
dappled sunlight, and unattended edging,
where blades of grass grow long and
tangle with their willing garden neighbors. This last
I give to God, who, breathing life upon the fields,
provides to those who've toiled.

I wake and gaze in starless midnight
and find that all my gifts are given.

DEPARTURE

As I walk to my car
with my head bent
to the angle of the sun—
one hundred degrees at 7pm—
I can see my sister
doing the same.

The same kind of lonely walk
away from a gathering,
knowing just how long it will be
until we see somebody—anybody—
again, bearing the inevitable
return to solitude
on shoulders that can
fold any minute.

I glance up and back down
for no other reason
than to shift the weight
of my sister's folded shoulders.

Somebody's artificial seagull
is flapping wildly over their rooftop
like a kite,
manufacturing turbulence
in the otherwise smooth evening air
as my shoes continue
to meet the pavement.

I open the door to my car
with my head bent
to the angle of the sun—
one hundred degrees at 7pm—
and my sister
does the same.

CRUEL LITTLE JOKES

The wind whips the trees at dusk.
Dark on dark, the leaves move
against the failed sky. I never saw her

as a blonde—spots of sunshine
in an uneasy mosaic,
popping like aneurysms, glints of blinding

light off a troubled lake. All these thoughts
of light as everything—
as it all—slips away, cruel little jokes

in locks of blonde hair. And tonight, dark
now merging into dark,
I'm much too wired to fight that cold morgue slab

I never visited.

IF IT GETS YOU DOWN

Tonight, I stumbled upon a piece of an old refrain:

Oh my, if it gets you down.

There was nothing else but the refrain itself: eight lines,
every other line is,

Oh my, if it gets you down.

Whatever the call, the same response. The same-as-always
stubbornness of the four walls which hold you.

Oh my, if it gets you down.

These walls take even the climbing, ratcheting of time,
nearly silent as it is, as a raucous enough call to echo.

Oh my, if it gets you down.

Simultaneously an admonishment of and permission to
fully embrace that which achieves your quickest destruction.

Oh my, if it gets you down.

Admission that it's an *urge* to dissolve. Dismissive only
insomuch as fighting the urge is contrary to the aim
of the urge itself.

Oh my, if it gets you down.

And there it is: the urge acts not *upon* you; you are all urge yourself, and there is no more split at hand than dissolution.

Give in.

Oh my, if it gets you down.

Give in.

Oh my, if it gets you down.

Give in.

RESPONSE

I

I speak to her in patterns of
enjambment

And she responds in
broken, halting cries

II

Long ago
the sound of childhood
harmlessly detonating over the sea

III

The cry of a hawk
pierced the stillness

It was cold outside,
but inside was tolerable

IV

It is always 5pm,
and I can't stop writing
about the wind

V

The first gentle brush
against a sleeping cheek,
the wind licked in curls
at eighty-five degrees,
is the year's first taste of fall,
but should we relish
the brief refreshment,
all the old excitement

VI

The snow covered the road,
an unbroken blanket
left to right

SILENCE, TONIGHT

Tonight,
silence eludes me.

My heart rails
at the cage
of stillness.

There is sunlight in everything—
roaring sunlight—
tearing at my clothing
like being dragged down
fully dressed.

I remember what it's like
not to breathe.

The air is baked from my lungs;
I feel the blood in my throat—
if only I could
gasp!
cry!
scream out a name,
any name!

O, God,
to whom I'll never pray,
you took away my life!

O, Love,
of whom I'll never dream,
you left me here to die!

O, Death,
with whom we cannot deal,
please let me breathe tonight

and swallow down
that tearing urge
to give away
the light.

STILL

Lately I am seeing mirages of danger
in the corners of my eyes. A glossy black spider
haltingly propelled on stabbing black spindles—
but no,

just a dark spot in the pattern on the tiles of the break room,
larger than the blotches surrounding it.
Decades-past commercial architecture and design
settle beneath my seat, and now it's 8:35,
so I lock the book back in my phone and walk
back to my desk.

And today a slowly creeping rattlesnake,
silent as death, rattle held calm, no warning
of the murder in its eye as it mounts my doorstep—
but still no,

a grayed root long since pushed above the surface
and worn down several layers and scarred.
And my head turned—perhaps it was
that I was reading Warren's "Rattlesnake Country,"
and the echoes of the higher-pitched notes
from the neighbor's air conditioner off the wall to my right
sounded to me like a rattle begrudgingly warning—
but still it was nothing.

And still I continue to turn.
It's scorching summer heat that follows me
wherever I go. It's a gnawing in my chest
that rolls and wakes me nightly, not like clockwork,
nothing so lovely and even. It's death
struck once too close and now I hide and hide
and hide, but death has no eyes, and I know this—
I know it smells me out like a dog sniffing out cancer—
but I've only ever learned to hide, and at least
hiding obscures my vision of the beast. And huddled
I crouch until I see it creeping again
in the corners of my eyes.

NEVERENDING

This afternoon, for whatever reason, it strikes me
that the air smells different on a Tuesday. Or maybe
it's just *this* Tuesday—a Tuesday so full of misplaced time.
The air is too warm for January, so I'm not freezing
in my bones, and this warmth is last year's lost summer.
Last year was never warm. The sun hung in the sky
as it always will—always enough for us, anyway—
but the light curved around us like we were holes
in the very fabric—curved around us and fell in,
but we were neverending holes. And now, this Tuesday
smells like fresh, warm laundry and the way grass feels
in dreams of childhood, and maybe this Tuesday isn't just
like any other day but—just possibly—it *is* any other day.

It's January and all the windows are open, but the air
is still and sits on either side of the window screens
like it was placed there—picked up from mid-May
and dropped at our doorsteps so that we feel it every time
we leave.

It's a summer that we thought tried so hard
to be itself and only struggled with its existence but in truth
it was afraid to start, as if that autumn would be the last,
and if we reached that point and all the fruit was ripe
and fell to the ground, it would rot there slowly in the air
and not even the bugs would carry it away because they knew
that even the harsh winds would find their end.

It's all the days when the sunset is nothing else but
tragedy, still orange and pink but you can imagine the red
beneath it, swallowing up the shadows below the horizon,
the ones that stretch forever, speckled only in the distance
by more tiny pink horizons.

It's early March and I'm not sitting down but lying
in bed having awoken late—with a few weeks yet left
of unemployment, still weary with that infinite freedom,
and it may have also been too warm but now certain details
fall away—and I answer my phone and my father says some words
that mean my sister is dead, that she killed herself last night,
and the two of us sit on either end of the phone as if our ears
are pressed together, and the light curves around us and falls in,
but we are neverending holes.

WITH THE REST OF THE TRAFFIC

She was carrying too many bags and kept
dropping her Smart Water. Really it was only
two bags, but even that's too many when it's
eighty-five heading toward one-oh-eight and maybe
your car's broke down and maybe you left it
in the parking lot of Somewhere or Another
because your grandparents have a car to hand down
out of the kindness of their hearts but just
haven't come through yet.

She was waiting for the light to tell her to cross
and the Smart Water kept clattering onto the
yellow grip pad with the bumps that keep you
from slipping on the slight decline from
the sidewalk to the street, but there was just
no more room for that bottle in those bags so she
shifted it under her arm as she picked up her
bags again and down went the Smart Water
like gravity had some kind of special hold on it.

She brushed back her dark hair, picked up the bottle
which had come from the gas station just one street
over, and held it, looking for the crossing signal
with an expression that didn't even remotely betray
the number of times she'd dropped that bottle
within the last twenty seconds. She had been pretty

when she was younger—that's what they'd said, as if
that was the world, as if that could decide for her
whether college was an option, whether divorce
would break her, if friends could replace family—and
she was young still, and pretty if you could look past
what her circumstances said about her.

And what they said was that gravity had some kind of
special hold on her. It held her feet more firmly
to the ground and made her legs heavy when she
walked and delivered a special kind of hurt when
she fell. It hurt her down in that place so deep
you swear it must be your soul, and the rest of us,
we don't see that hurt; we can't see down to it past the
bags filled with what must be God-knows-what
and that bottle that won't fit anywhere in them and
her feet planted unmoving on that yellow grip pad.

The light turned green and I eased forward and
passed her with the rest of the traffic. She
continued to wait, and the bottle continued to
clatter to the sidewalk, and I lost sight of whether
she continued to pick it up.

ABOUT THE AUTHOR

Ryan Kenneth Allen is the author of two previous collections of poetry: *Mold* (2019) and *Reflections and Falling and Loving What's Lost* (2020). He currently lives in Northern California with his fiancé and their dog.

www.ingramcontent.com/pod-product-compliance
Lightning Source LLC
LaVergne TN
LVHW050943080826
845145LV00004B/1391

* 9 7 8 1 7 3 5 6 3 6 4 3 6 *